THE PROPHETESS

THE
PROPHETESS

THE RETURN of THE PROPHET
from THE VOICE of the DIVINE FEMININE

CHELAN HARKIN

HAY HOUSE LLC
Carlsbad, California • New York City
London • Sydney • New Delhi

Published in the United States by: Hay House LLC: www.hayhouse.com˚
Published in Australia by: Hay House Australia Publishing Pty Ltd:
    www.hayhouse.com.au
Published in the United Kingdom by: Hay House UK Ltd: www.hayhouse.co.uk
Published in India by: Hay House Publishers (India) Pvt Ltd: www.hayhouse.co.in

Cover design: Barbara LeVan Fisher
Interior design: Claudine Mansour Design
Interior illustration: "Noli Timere" by Thomas Benedikt Stern,
    @thomasbenediktstern, thomasbenediktstern.com

The author of this book does not dispense medical advice or prescribe the use of any technique as a form of treatment for physical, emotional, or medical problems without the advice of a physician, either directly or indirectly. The intent of the author is only to offer information of a general nature to help you in your quest for emotional, physical, and spiritual well-being. In the event you use any of the information in this book for yourself, the author and the publisher assume no responsibility for your actions.

Cataloging-in-Publication Data is on file at the Library of Congress

Trade Paperback ISBN: 978-1-4019-7756-6
E-book ISBN: 978-1-4019-7757-3
Audiobook ISBN: 978-1-4019-7758-0
10 9 8 7 6 5 4 3 2 1
1st edition, September 2024

Printed in the United States of America

This product uses responsibly sourced papers and/or recycled materials. For more information, see www.hayhouse.com.

*My daughter Nahanni
and Kahlil Gibran*

*"A little while, a moment of rest upon the wind,
and another woman shall bear me."*

— from *The Prophet* by Kahlil Gibran

CONTENTS

THE ADORATION

Foreword by Daniel Ladinsky

In reading over some pages again in this book this morning, it seemed that the very gifted poet, Chelan Harkin, is offering the world some revelations of great utility via her words.

The impetus behind the movements and thoughts of all creatures is both nourishment and freedom. Freedom from what we don't want to feel, like fear and suffering, and the freedom to embrace, to hold within our eyes or touch, some aspects of beauty, (and nature can be as wondrously beautiful as it is loving).

And helping to satisfy within us this quest for well-being and the desire for fun—what might help you sing and dance more, what might help you to sit more quietly at times, what can make you more generous and kind to others and to yourself, what can encourage and hone your talents as well as safeguard and empower you—those are some of the vital aspects—words—of the true teacher, prophet, or prophet-ess. Those are the words of a real friend.

And the creative presentation of such words: the sacred understanding or compassion in them, and their wonderful desire and duty to help a wing on your spirit more unfurl and taste the sky—to taste God—that is what has drawn millions to the work of Khalil Gibran. That is what has drawn millions, for centuries, to the poems of Rumi and Hafiz—and hopefully, now, to this significant book by Chelan.

The Adoration. Let that be a litmus test of any true teacher of any great literature. How much can they set you upon the holy throne where we are all in line, destined to be crowned, to become so aware of the miracle of existence, that once we are, we could be truly satisfied forever with just the astounding movement of our own hand—truly satisfied with anything that ever was, or could be, or is. We come, then, to know the Magnif-icent Luminous Sovereignty that is the soul of our heart.

But often, that divine awareness can surely seem a long way off, and even beyond one's imagination. Yet the rivers, all forms, and us, are moving toward that radiant ocean of omni-presence. And this is a book that can lead one toward that radiance. I hope you sit with the pages in this book and can feel adored and helped.

There are gold mines in some of these pages and words. So much so that I would suggest reading what is here slowly and out loud, being as present as you can, 'cause ...

consciously walking

buddha tickles

feet

Aka: *The Prophetess* can smooch ya. And as ironic as it may seem, slowing down at times can crank the party way up and increase your applause both of life and your wondrous self. Hey, The Adoration.

It is an honor to have been asked to write the foreword to this book. And I'll bet the angels and the mountains thank Chelan for her work.

—DANIEL LADINSKY

International best-selling poet and author

danielladinsky.com

INTRODUCTION

To write a book framed as the continuation of *The Prophet*, the classic, globally beloved book by Kahlil Gibran is a surreal, exhilarating, and unmatched honor.

I have loved and felt deep reverence for *The Prophet* since I was a young girl. A worn copy stood on my parents' bookshelf. I was always aware of its power. Looking back, it is clear that I always esteemed Kahlil's book as one of a kind, as a deeply sacred text. I felt it to carry an energy of authentic love that inspired, attracted and deeply intrigued me. It was clear to me that *The Prophet* held a quality that was rare, precious, and alive.

The Prophet emanates an inspired articulation of reality that offered perhaps my first experience of how words could be a tool to craft a home and a place of deep belonging for a dimension of being that is essential but all too rarely recognized and acknowledged.

As with a harmony to a melody, *The Prophet* seemed to carry a tone, a frequency, that added a richness and a dimension to traditional spiritual understandings.

I want to share with you the extraordinary story of how I came to be the author of *The Prophetess*. I want to share with you how this book came to be and to let you in on the story of my connection with Kahlil Gibran.

Toward the end of 2020 I was preparing to self-publish my first book of mystical poetry, Susceptible to Light. Close to its publication date I experienced an unusual and irresistible inner prompting to experiment with praying to my favorite dead poets for marketing support. Hafiz and Kahlil Gibran were elected chairmen of what I called my A-Team. Though I had no contacts in the marketing world and only one contact in the publishing world (at least on the material plane) I was seized by a powerful desire for my book to reach many in the name of love, truth, and liberation. I approached this prayer experiment with an attitude of, "Nothing to lose. Why not give this a shot?"

I had never prayed like this before, wholeheartedly, vulnerably, genuinely. It felt beautiful, quirky, and strange. These prayers were playful, honest, intimate, a bit awkward, experimental, sincere, and involved asking for what I most truly desired.

Each night I would put my small children to bed, make myself a rich cup of hot chocolate, put on some flashy earrings for ceremonial flair and walk around my block praying to my dead poets in the sky. Almost as soon as this prayer experiment began, what had previously been a steady flow of poetic inspiration became torrential. I was flooded with inspiration. Not more than a week into this experiment and right before my first book was released, a poem came through that went wildly viral. My audience of about 20 at the most, that was often just my mom and her three supportive friends, became a global audience overnight.

Not more than three weeks into the launch of that book, something remarkable happened that has lastingly and indelibly changed my life and my understanding of reality. In late December of 2020, I received an email in my inbox from Daniel Ladinsky, the renderer of Hafiz poetry, one of the world's most successful living poets and my primary poetic inspiration.

He asked me if I knew who he was and introduced himself as a reclusive poet in Taos who rarely reached out to anyone but saw my book and felt a strange nudge to reach out to me. That I had been praying to Hafiz for marketing support and was now in contact with Daniel Ladinsky, the man who has created the most wide-spread renderings of Hafiz poetry to the English-speaking world, was beyond belief. I responded to him in quite an unprofessional manner, sharing my almost unhinged ecstasy about the circumstances along with the details of this story. The second email he sent me was an invitation to co-author a book with him.

In that moment, some deep cork in the heart of reality was yanked. Everything shone with effervescence and became intoxicated with wonder. A deep part of my being has not been sober since. Daniel's idea was for our book to be a collection of inspired letters written back and forth. I told him that I'd also been praying to Kahlil Gibran and suggested we style our book similarly to *The Prophet*, sharing thematic letters on meaningful themes. He then told me he had written the foreword to the extended edition of *The Prophet*. And he has now written the foreword to *The Prophetess*.

Not more than a month into our correspondence, Daniel, with his generous style and poetic brilliance, endorsed me to some of the major publishing houses in the world, Hay House and Penguin Random House included. I could not believe my fortune.

Roughly a year and a half following all of this, I had just put my kids to bed and was drawing a bath when I was hit with a sort of lightning bolt of the clearest knowing. Energy moves through me as inspired poetry, and this was similar to that but amped up louder, clearer and with more voltage. Were the force that moved through me at that moment to have been given voice, it would have said,

"It is time to write *The Prophetess* and you are the one to do it."

Immediately content started to cascade through me. The core of a few of this book's chapters were written in that night alone. Not more than two months later I had written most of the content of the entire book. It truly did feel like it was time, and it was ready to pour.

The creating of this book mostly took place in the forest where I would go on walks and ask Kahlil for inspiration. What I heard from him every time was, "Let it be easeful, Chelan. Don't overwrite it. You have years and years of exploration into the nature of reality and the human condition. This book is to be made with joy." I felt him with me in an intimate way throughout this process. This book is written in the deepest love, honor, and homage to him.

Thank you for receiving my story that has been quite an odyssey of my emergence and remaking. This book is offered as a bow to Kahlil Gibran. And I bow to the forces of reality that make magic happen when we ask them to with alignment and an open heart.

I recently learned that the year my proposal was accepted by Hay House, 2023, was the 100th year anniversary of the publishing of The Prophet. I also learned that Kahlil Gibran was inspired by the Baha'i Writings. I was struck by this having grown up in a Baha'i home. The last chapter of Kahlil Gibran's beloved book is largely a prophecy of his return. The final line of his masterpiece says, "A little while, a moment upon the wind, and another woman shall bear me."

With the deepest gratitude,
in the name of the continuation of awe,
Chelan Harkin

THE TIME OF THE END

The oil was running low in the lamp of the world's chest. The flower of its poetry needed water. Life had become more a series of chores than an unfoldment of wonders, more a list than a song. Something verdant and alive in the human spirit had been forgotten.

What prayer is brave enough to reach its hopes through the cold despondency of winter to try again to summon spring? What supplication leads the parched throat of the desert to finally evoke rain? Is there a final flower that offers itself up from the almost barren heart, that finally opens grace? It is a furious thirst for reality that says our most persuasive prayers.

In this case, an ancient and finally unbearable tension of longing in the soul of the world invoked Her. She was summoned like the warm call of the South the soul of a bird. She came like a migration of light to the heart.

She came like the sun, a disruption to the darkness both natural and alarming to the orientation of the past. She was the deepest bewilderment to those who had for so long used the compass of the old. They had become embedded in the dark, and to them, dawn had become a dream.

But the prow of Her ship cut through the long-hung veil of this night. She was a sword of light. She was a balm to everything.

Her ship docked. She didn't pause, She didn't wait. Like the sun, She didn't ask permission to rise. It was time. The bell had rung in the hearts. People gathered as She entered the square, pulled by an irresistible attraction to something of the revelation of their own destiny She seemed to hold within Her.

She, She, She.

What was *She?* She was impossible for understanding to contain. She was not a fragment. She was entirety. And She directly and unswervingly spoke to and activated our entirety.

She was the Substance of Mystery, The Artisan of the New, The Cartographer of Consciousness. She challenged and confronted everything in our hearts that kept us apart from ourselves and enticed and galvanized us to enter the mapless wildlands of the new frontiers of love—That place our old ideologies could not chart, that place for which the guidance of the past could give us no assurance and the place toward which we were irresistibly impelled. My God, realized the hearts in the crowd, gaping and stunned, The Authority of Love had returned *as a woman*—*The Prophetess* has arrived.

She spoke, and Her voice was a cascade of stars.

I bring in the wings of my chest the time of the end. It is seeded with the time of the new. To enter one is to enter both. The time of the end is the end of the belief of our unworthiness. It is the end of separation. I am here to chart the path from separation to wholeness. This is the age of reclamation.

Nothing that I bring have you not asked for. I am not here to teach you. I am here to enunciate your knowing, to breathe confidence into the intimations in your soul. I am the manifestation of your hidden prayers. I am here to pour holy oil on your light. Old ways of being that no longer serve have made this world a tinderbox. It's time to set it aflame with the wild grace of the awakening truth in your hearts.

We are great mystery in human form. There's a land in the soul that we all dream of and long for. The soul is always in prayer for reunion with this place. It holds something of a jasmine fragrance whose perfume keeps calling us. I live in this land that has called to you and perplexed you, the land where we become beautiful, fresh, and alive again. It is the land beyond control, the land of surrender, that contains all you've sought. This land resides within you, too, with equal stature and majesty. This is the place in you to which I shall speak. I am in service to your nobility.

We are not alive to survive. We are alive to know the most profound intimacy of the deathless soul. We are alive to unfold the sensitivities of our knowing that we might touch the vivid and tender cheek of reality.

It is time to redefine everything that our patterns may come to support the flourishing of the human spirit. We are the creative agents of reality, not passive recipients of history's long-dead traditions.

There is an invisible movement happening of which you are all a part. It is time to participate more fully. We are all co-creators in the awakening of human consciousness. The latent period of human dormancy is over. It is time to bring all of ourselves to light. This is the era of inclusion. Nothing in ourselves can any more be cast out, rejected. The new world is the world of complete embrace. This is the age of wholeness.

What of us will remain when we cross this threshold into the new? The new paradigm has nothing to do with domination, with judgments of good or bad, right or wrong as we've known it. It is about learning the mechanics of authentic closeness. Separation, what does this world look like when we stop worshipping you as our primary God? We are being prepared to live this answer.

AWAKENING

Speak to us of awakening. And *The Prophetess* spoke,

It's okay if you're scared when you're opening. The seed, she was scared too. Do you think the coal wanted to become a diamond? She was scared out of her wits of change—It took her 10 thousand years to even be able to pray for it. The acorn was so closed in by the hard walls of his staunch beliefs. Oh, how he protested becoming the regal, generous oak. Have you heard the caterpillar's shrieks of resistance as some bigger force unwelcomely impels it to eat its own form while disclosing nothing of those secret wings?

The only difference in us from them is we have an even more stubborn resistance. But ultimately, we are impelled by the same irresistible force to completely self-destruct into a new and improved yet to be discovered marvel. Do your best to allow this—You, too, were made for wings.

Awakening is a profoundly humble affair. And true humility and true power are one. For to access true power is to connect with the fullness of yourself. It is to hide from and reject nothing of yourself. It is to make yourself a hollow reed through which Life's wisdoms can flow.

We need a more holistic, humanized, and embodied understanding of awakening, one that doesn't tempt us toward the seductive illusion of suffering's end. Awakening helps us into a new, healthier relationship with suffering—One that no longer identifies with it or puts us apart from it, but rather allows us to directly enter its heart. The process of awakening is to be able to fully feel rather than flee. Here, we find there is an old world inside us all whose wreckage is mercy. There is a way through each wound and a new temple awaits you at the bottom of your deepest tears.

Often the temple of awakening is the hollow bone of loneliness. Its opening is often found by those who experience unlivable anguish in the cramped conditions of the closed heart and must break open to the risk of wider possibility.

When frailties bleed out and there's no balm to grab save the salve of surrender, awakening doesn't so much close the wound as give purpose to its pouring. Life's fruits often bloom from being such a barren snag that you must graft parts of yourself to God. We must be careful, lest we elevate anyone for anything holy they produce or make awakening into something that sets some above others. More often than not, any wisdom or insight that can truly reach a heart comes from those whose wounds have become so unbearable, they must burst into song.

Awakening is messy. You don't transcend into some paradisiacal, elitist inner garden. It doesn't perfect you. You first come into all of the reasons you've so wanted to stay asleep. And there are many very good reasons. We awaken to all the rea- sons we've so wanted to disassociate from our bodies—Those storehouses of mortality and God where to enter through either door is to have stripped from you the illusion of smallness.

Sleeping is relatively painless, in its numbed way. To awaken, really, is to begin to feel. As we feel through more pain, we feel more compassion. Awakening is, bit by bit, coming out of denial around all the reasons we've needed to wield that terrible tool of othering. It is diving into the cracks in our hearts rather than mortaring them and staying long enough to build kinship with all that was once unbearable inside of our own self.

It does not look like being perfectly empowered, seamlessly composed—It is to commit with all our hearts to no longer take out our helplessness on anyone else.

Awakening isn't characterized by arrival at a stern, stoic, at last invulnerable spirituality. It doesn't come from spiritual mastery defined as overcoming enough of our shortcomings. Rather, it is found in doing our fumbling best to grow into arms strong and loving enough to hold all of our aching humanity.

Awakening is the at times compassless and often inglorious inner odyssey toward the rough ruby of all that is bruised and true in our hearts.

Awakening isn't only for special people. We're all on our way toward coming out of the sleep cycle. Be not fooled: the myth that awakening looks anything like spiritual perfectionism is perhaps the best sleeping pill.

VULNERABILITY

Speak to us of vulnerability. And *The Prophetess* spoke,

Vulnerability is bravery incarnate. It is the holy gateway into the wholeness of the heart. To be vulnerable is to unlock access to what is real and true and alive inside of us—The hurt and the holy, the tender and the triumphant. It is to at last return connection to these places we so thought we needed to condemn.

Vulnerability is self-sacrifice. And to sacrifice means to make sacred. In vulnerability we sacrifice our unsustainable, partial, performed self for true connection. Vulnerability moves us beyond the isolated misery of rank and conquest. When we expose truths inside of our hearts that we fear will lessen our value, injure our competitive odds at getting resources or social esteem, we are engaging in a profound act of making sacred our heart space and our relational space. What we sacrifice in vulnerability is the paradigm of self-preservation, competition, and separation. In this we embark on the sacred passage into the paradigm of wholeness and belonging.

The expression of vulnerability is the process of self-liberation. We are freeing that which we have long rejected. We need to hold each other in the highest esteem and honor as we become willing to risk opening the pain of our past for the possibility of our full presence.

It is not through overcoming our pain that one heals and discovers satisfaction. It is through being willing to relate to our pain differently, in a way that finally allows connection to come to it. To open vulnerably confronts every old narrative by taking the great, revolutionary risk that the wounds of our past might be assets to belonging rather than liabilities.

Vulnerability is disarmed truth. Through it we step into greater inner coherence as we come out of the miserable vow to the dissonance of hiding. Vulnerability is the coronation of the heart, the consecration of relationship. Our access to divinity is as deep as our access to humility.

Rather than being weak, fussy, pathetic or fragile, vulnerability is a radical act and radical means of the roots. To express vulnerably is really to have the courage and wisdom to excavate and express the truth of an emotion. An emotion that starts out as an angry weapon in the hands of the invulnerable, when expressed with the disarmament of vulnerably, is traced to its transformational, accountable, reconnective root that sutures relational rupture and re-opens intimacy. Intimacy is vulnerability's jewel.

This great act enriches the beggar and impels the king to bow. Together, in this act that honors the greater wholeness of both, they become more than either could ever lose or gain.

We must make haste to renounce any idea that vulnerability is anything less than potent courage. Without vulnerability, we live outside of the heart, in the margins of life. Here, we are poor indeed and spend our days blindly scraping at the world for the satisfaction we can only find in the depths of our openness.

Embrace the God who prefers to fall to His knees and weep over the God who wants to posture His frailties as wrath.

In vulnerability, our humanity and our divinity are redeemed in each other. The heart, when opened honestly, becomes a sanctuary for all humanity that gives rest to the terrible burden of loneliness. The blunt and sobering truth is there is no path to deep, relational satisfaction outside of the path of the open heart. The only way to know and be known, and to have the possibility to trust and be deeply trusted is to share both the divine and the destitute, the ravishing and the unruly, the holy and the hollow inside of us.

Alas, we win nothing from shielding our hearts from each other. My dears, vulnerability can be terrifying. But we must learn to go, like a dark prayer, down and in to find the tap-root of our truth.

My dears, resisting the open heart cannot last. We must grow in strength to surrender to it.

TRUTH

Speak to us of truth. And *The Prophetess* spoke,

There are worn-out social conventions that desperately need to be destroyed by whatever truth is in your heart. The specific flavor of truth tonic kept hidden in the apothecary of your chest is exactly the medicine this world needs. It is time to bring it forth. You, my dear, are good medicine, and the truths within you have been prescribed for this time.

Truth is a sacred interruption of conditioned blindness. It empowers everyone and enables no one. Truth leverages nothing against anyone and calls people up into all they might be.

We are all healers and creators by being our truest selves. Unspoken truth is at the base of all our relational pain. Unspoken truth is at the base of all worn-out patterns we would rather maintain than transform.

To bring truth forward moves us from self-preservation to self-transformation. It bursts through unstable foundations that could only hold the unsustainable.

Truth is the supreme liberator. And what liberates one supports the liberation of all. To liberate means to free our hearts from the limited bondage of conditional love. What is unspoken within us contains us.

Cultivate a thirst for truth that nothing else can slake. In alignment with our truth, the reeds of our destiny quiver with the music of the cosmos. The path of truth is our redemption, our renaissance, our resurrection, and our remaking. It clarifies our essence.

Truth is unconquerable. It is powerful without any desire to overpower, and in its absolute dominion it requires no defense. What is untruthful is unsustainable. For what is sustainable will last and what will last will ascend and what will ascend is the powerfully authentic expression of Life that is beneficial to the flourishing of all.

While truth can bring the discomfort of shaking you out of the comfortable narcotic of falsity, truth never harms.

Truth restores us with the most personal and universal intimacy with our essence. Walk with truth and let others be invited to deepen themselves in their reception of you.

We all need to take the sword of truth from its sheath of silence. It is time to slay illusion, not with violence but with the blade of clarity, of discernment. Truth is ever only wielded in the name of and by the hands of love. Truth germinates our reality to break through the hard seed of our conditioning, it calls forth our potential. If love is the beauty of the flower, truth is the boldness that brings it to continuously reveal more of itself.

FEELINGS

Speak to us of feelings. And *The Prophetess* spoke,

This is a feeling universe. Do you think the wild rose opens for intellectual reasons? Or does it have more to do with needing to finally feel the kiss of the sun in the center of her wide-open chest?

Emotion is the ancient language of Life. We become fluent in our being's mother tongue as we learn the value and utility of feeling. Emotion means energy in motion. Our feelings are part of Life's great, inbuilt communication system to us. This energy, when we let it flow, carries information, insight, inspiration, and the wisest, truest guidance for our lives.

What we deny in ourself—hideous or beautiful—destroys us. What we embrace in ourself—hideous of beautiful—brings us to blossom. This is the age of embrace.

Feelings are the varied tones of Life's energies. These vital energies are the greatest gifts to our edification as we allow ourself to receive them.

For millennia, feelings have been feared, rejected, repressed. Why? When we truthfully and openly acknowledge and feel through our feelings, we release all the strategies of control that have kept us small, disempowered and separate. When we feel our feelings, our bound energy is freed and we move beyond our limiting contracts to our old conditioning. Feelings have been feared and shunned as great spiritual teachers have been feared and shunned—They are tremendous revolutionaries of freedom, unmatched agents of transformation.

What has made emotions challenging is simply our judgments about them. In our lack of familiarity with our feelings, we have repressed and mishandled them. It is the disconnection from our emotions that causes disturbance in their expression.

Our judgments have made us illiterate in what could otherwise be our deepest gift—To constructively commune with and channel the flow of Life.

Feelings are not contrary to spirituality, but essential, foundational. Feelings are the continuous stream of brilliance that comes from our Source. They want to flow through us. Each of these energies carries a gift. There is no "bad" or "wrong" energy. Energy is potential, and what we do with it can catalyze the light of the world.

We are not our feelings. We are their stewards. But to not identify with our feelings does not mean we do not have them. To have feelings is not a sign of being immature or undeveloped. How we relate to our feelings is what reflects our level of development. Our societal shame stories about feelings are the embodied dams we place on Life that stunt our growth and cramp our joy.

Neither should we repress nor project our feelings. We must become responsible and skilled feelers, able, willing and resilient enough to feel through all that is not love, truth, and humility.

The collection of pain you hold from your past is the assignment granted to you by humanity's destiny. If related to rightly, releasing our trapped, deeply held emotions is the surest way for Life's energies to evolve through us toward ever-widening iterations of more mature love.

The strong are they who responsibly feel instead of weaponize their feelings. Our bodies are not arsenals. Rather than stay a minion of fear that protects the storehouse of our past, when we make contact with our most uncomfortable feelings, we become empowered agents of our destiny.

There is a temple in the wound and a holy land in the broken heart. Stored history that doesn't serve you is meant to be cleansed through the holy baptism of catharsis in the chapel of your chest.

To feel through any feeling will teach you the ways of no longer conquering your tenderness. To know we can feel through anything grants us the resilience to no longer hide from Life or mask our innocence. It empowers us to lean in toward Life more genuinely with a heart that is more disarmed. For it is not the circum- stances in Life we fear but our feelings about them. As we learn that even the hardest feelings yield extraordinary gifts when we stay with them with patience and presence, what else have we to fear?

Like a heavy sky that will never discontinue being filled with the weighty blessings of rain, the heart longs to open again to pour in a way that enlivens all the earth in its great, surrendered release of sorrow. And as the sunshine of remembrance spreads its wide, golden arms in your chest, it becomes clear again—The clouds, too, were God.

INTIMACY

Speak to us of intimacy. And *The Prophetess* spoke,

Intimacy is to desire for your heart the pangs of closeness over the pangs of distance. It begins with the heart's great recognition that it did not come to this Earth to be a mere acquaintance of love. Intimacy begins when our deep soul says, "I no longer want to hurt in private. I no longer want to keep God at arm's length. I want to stop the harsh demands that I must clean myself up first and see if I can allow love to flood the entirety of my beautiful and broken heart."

Intimacy is to reinstate a God that feels like a sister holding you on your worst days. It is to know there is a tender holiness in life that you are made of and to whom you belong.

Collect all the sweet stars into your chest tonight—Darling, don't you know we can be this close and vast? Yes, the great magnitude of our love is what the Universe is expanding into.

To know intimacy is to know you deeply belong to Life. That the inclusive congregation of stars whose only doctrine is "Shine" wants your heart as a member and the community of hillside daisies considers you an integral part. Find your soulmate winking out at you through every ordinary moment and remember that each night the moon sets her light in the sky to encourage and applaud your radiance.

Set upon the path of renouncing what has kept your heart calloused from closeness. Intimacy is the consecration of truth in the other through the great witnessing of its preciousness.

Enter the chamber in the heart where God undresses Herself through revealing every luminous vulnerability. Full access to your secret trove of tenderness is Life's primary desire.

Intimacy will show you every wall you've held around your heart that must be let down for the fullness of love's entrance. It is the great breach into all of the protective strategies and security systems around our tenderness—Do all you can to allow this.

We long for and hide from intimacy in almost equal measure. We fear intimacy's rejection would be our undoing and its close embrace would be our remaking.

Say, "yes" to this closeness with Life and intimacy will uncork your crown chakra and pour God through you. You will become sodden with music, dripping with poetry, and longing for more of yourself to share with your beloved. Intimacy is a treasure map. Touched by it, the soul plunders the abundance of life—Each atom becomes a jewel.

Say, "yes" to this closeness with Life and intimacy will pollinate you with longing and leave you with no rest. It exposes your distance to and longing for the inmost heart of God and leaves you desperate to find refuge there. Intimacy agitates a wild reverence in your soul to such a degree that you cannot, even for one moment, stop singing the name of your longing.

If the house of your soul has felt vacant for too long, ask that all your doors be opened and for light to enter every room of you at once. When the mundanities of living without The Beloved are exposed, there's no true returning to this distant rock of a world. For intimacy is a threat and a promise to undo you of every safe remoteness by putting the sun in your heart and unlocking all verdure and holiness.

Let Life take your hand and move you from the distant and conceptual into the profoundly relatable. Stop thinking about God—Cry your heart out. Stop your dry, prim talks with

God—She doesn't desire those boring meetings. Wake up at midnight and write Her love poems with star ink. God's tired of the same position with prayer; lie down on the forest floor and drink Her in through your pores.

You are a pilgrim on beauty's path that leads you ever deeper into the Beloved's eternal heart that always beats within you.

RELATIONSHIP

Speak to us of relationship. And *The Prophetess* spoke,

We are here to bring forth our light and hold the candles of ourselves to each other.

If we're honest, most don't want an aloof, abstract spirituality that lives in the stars. What most long for is a path that endows us with ever deeper resources to be strong and compassionate enough to stay in relationship with the vulnerabilities, complexes, difficulties, and great beauties within the human heart.

And few of us are motivated by God or goodness or growth for their own sake. Mostly we are seeking the reassurance of our worthiness to enter the irresistible crucible of the holy wreckage of human relationship.

Relationship is love's servant. In devotion to the light, relationship builds the lamp. Love is the energy, the electricity. Relationship is that which catalyzes its light into the world.

We need each other—End of story. And there is no shame in this. It is beautiful, it is a necessity, it is a truth. The difference between co-dependent need and healthy need is that co-dependent need enables each other's hiding. Healthy need recognizes that we need each other for our full emergence. Kiss all of those emissaries of The Nameless One, those in your life who bring you to your knees and lead you back to yourself.

Each deep love, especially with a primary partner, activates the lack and longing from our past. If we use the gift of this invitation to resolve our lack, we have the possibility of realizing—of bringing to life—the fruits of our longing.

It is a deep resignation to become tired of each other. Darling—There are universes inside each other ever being born.

Too often, relationship becomes a form of protest, a form of resistance, or demand around something unresolved or unreceived from our past. Do all you can to creatively boycott this. Stage a sit-in in your own heart to see what needs to be done to restore yourself to your natural condition of love's plenty.

Know that any competition is naught but pain sparring against pain, which only adds to itself. And conflict, even when well disguised as the noble defense of truth, is not but scarcity's perpetuation. The seeming oneness that goes to war for itself still wields separation's weapon. To love is not to cunningly win. Nor is it to leverage any advantage of self-perpetuation over the other.

Within love is a seed and a wrecking ball. The seed blossoms into suns and the wrecking ball destroys old worlds. From it a new self emerges.

Let your relationship be one that relieves you of your well-packaged cleverness. Tell your beloved you have a million wounds you won't use against them.

May your heart's prayer to its beloved be this: that as you go from me, as you one day inevitably will, and as I go from you, let us go in the grace of love's completion that never held back anything of itself.

LOVE

Speak to us of love. And *The Prophetess* spoke,

We are all here on this Earth for the great work of love, and love is not for the faint of heart. We are each a tall, mighty tree inside of a small seed—Love is what breaks us open. Love is the systematic destroyer of every small self as it calls us forth into all we're destined to be.

Love is the true evolutionary force in this Universe—The only thing we desire enough to grow beyond ourself.

Love is the only thing persuasive enough to convince us to take on the mad and harrowing voyage from bud to blossom. And that said, I hope you can let her in to do her sacred, reckless thing to the heart of your life anyway.

Besides love, what reason have the atoms to be bound together? What other motivation have the planets to whirl around that dazzling light? Love is the deepest law of the universe. Love is the origin, the destination, and the medium of all things. The truth, my dear—*Busy yourself with naught else, for there is nothing but love.*

With love, eternity is infused into every otherwise mortal moment.

For your own sake, don't commit the grievous ignorance of shallowing yourself and love by demanding that love be comfortable. Let her sear and singe and be the reason why you grow. For love is not meant to spare us from our necessary suffering that brings us to blossom. Love is meant to captivate us so much that we're willing to successively move through ever-deeper levels of old limitations as we more closely approach the reality of the authentic heart.

Love is for your joy and your emergence. And also let love be a sanctuary for your sorrows that they may rest while they pass through you on their path back to their final destination, which is also love.

We often demand of another in the name of love that they protect rather than reveal our wounds. But love is the path of the progressively uncovered heart. And while love will reveal your wounds, it will also kneel by their side to join you with absolute tenderness as you cleanse them together with deeper understanding.

At each threshold into the deeper heart, the lover has the choice to fight, flee, or bow. To love is to continually bow your pain before the preciousness you feel in each other. Those who are willing to bow beneath their deepest fears are those who let *The Artist of The Unknown* draw ever deeper and finer iterations of their love. Again and again we must be willing to die to ourselves, ever deeper, for our love to be remade.

Spare yourself from all knowledge but the knowledge of love—The love that edifies the mountains, the love that makes the oak grow into the full nobility of itself, the love that gives the robin its song. Spare yourself from all but the love that cloaks each night with elegance, that writes poetic eloquence into life, the love that is the mother tongue of all hearts that speaks with the fluency of oneness.

See not pain and love as separate. For to live a full and present life is for love to be the attendant at the bedside of each of our wounds. To say pain and love are separate is to do that unloving thing of splitting life by telling one experience it needs to change before it is worthy of love. The great redemption of our pain is reunion with love. And love, in her great absence of judgment, shares herself unconditionally with anything that would benefit from her presence.

The depth of our ability to love reveals the depth of our ability to lose. To lose is love's inevitability but our choice lies in how beautifully we lose. In this great art of loss, that is love, our hearts are called to unforeseen depths of courage. To stand at the base of love's great mountain is to enter into a profound consultation with the truth in our hearts about what we're willing to lay down of ourself on love's path. If we are willing to lose for love's blossoming, rather than lose in the protection of love's hiding, the eternal is grown no matter what becomes dust.

This world was always only made of love. Stay close to whatever in this world allows you to reveal its original form.

THE FEMININE

Speak to us of The Feminine. And *The Prophetess* spoke,

We often sorely mistake The Feminine for a pretty and graceful fair maiden or a Goddess of only nurturance who, subservient to our comforts, decorates our lives, sings to us, and feeds us only our ease.

But The Feminine is a three-headed Goddess made of Truth, Justice, and Power from within. She breathes the fire of dominion and radical acceptance, and while She is always loving, She is rarely comfortable. She is not here to castrate or emasculate men but to help them claim their crown. And She does not only abide in women—She abides in the human soul. She is the eco-warrior who unapologetically bursts through the dams blocking you from the vitality of your grief. She is what will not stay small and tidy and polite to keep you from the immeasurable fullness of your life.

The Feminine is shorthand for the great divine force that lives within you, that wants to restore you to your inner power, that comes from embracing your wholeness. She wants to exonerate and ennoble your messy, imperfect, scuffed, glorious, and completely essential humanity. She bursts through ideological pavings that have covered our soul's knowing to introduce us to the embodied God who is not afraid to roar or weep. She is the revolutionary who will undo conquering consciousness that represses so much of ourselves and has sickened and made limp the heart of our world. She is intolerant of our separation from ourselves to please the old dogma of conditional love. We are malnourished in our continuous competition with others for the resources we first reject in ourself. She wants us well fed.

She is the primordial form of the holy word "No" that begins forming in our gut, in our hips, in the deepest furrows of our knowing. She is what will not tolerate the denigration of human worth and inherent dignity. She is the toppler of the terrible illusion of hierarchy.

She is the marvelous unraveller of the status quo, that corset stifling the deep breath of society's truth. She is gloriously irreverent to all falsities that make God out to be anything but the infinite embrace of your entirety. She is the wisdom and life stored in your pain that will not stop howling until you stop your busy life to kneel by her side and find value in the voice you once learned to silence.

The Feminine is here to crack open your body, women and men and all, to finally release the poison of every ancient, uncleaned wound.

The Feminine is here to crack open your old ideologies and shoot new life through you like a seed hard and closed for so many years and suddenly kissed into transformation by the great destruction of light.

The Feminine is here to pull you from the measured, surveyed land at the edge of the wild forest of your dreams and finally toss you into that mapless territory of your heart.

The Feminine is here to remind you that God can live in the earth, in the hips, in the deepest shadows. She reminds us that God is planted like a wild rose in the darkest furrows of your pain to teach you to mother your frailties rather than dominate them and bring the wound from exile into embrace.

The Feminine is here to reunite tenderness with power and to help you source this from the great, hidden sea within—She wants you to feel the intimacy of God pulsing Her embodied song through the rivers of your blood and back to the holy ocean of your heart.

The Feminine is here to tell us in no uncertain terms that though we have tried to bury Her, we are in the process of Her great resurrection. She has been buried in our bodies, but our bodies are not burial grounds but birthing rooms. She has been gestating there. We are carrying Her ancient wisdom, and a great, never-before-seen beauty is soon due to be born.

SIN

Speak to us of sin. And *The Prophetess* spoke,

Of all the false names for God, start by throwing out "Judge." God has no podium, no gavel. She longs to celebrate you, to sing to you, to kiss you awake. The structure She wants for our lives is that which will support our growing happiness, more a trellis than a hard, restricting set of laws.

To sin, essentially, means to not drink in as much light as you possibly could have.

The straight and narrow? That notion may go. This life is an ever-widening unfoldment of your luminosity. It is time to step outside the bounds of the linear march toward salvation and begin to see God as a dancing spiral that encompasses all creation.

II am not suggesting moral anarchy. I am telling you we need to move from a harsh, judgment-based, ideological morality to an authentic morality that recognizes we are animated by Life's natural goodness. I am telling you that there is innocence at the root of our missteps—Not an innocence that bypasses accountability but an essential innocence, the recognition of which makes us brave enough to be accountable. I am telling you that institutional models of fear and shame perpetuate sin, and that sin comes from pain that hasn't been able to find belonging.

That said, if you think the Eccentric God who made the octopus is going to judge you for your sins, I'm afraid you've missed the mark. If you think this Wild God who spins galaxies as a pastime cares to get fussy about your mistakes or has ever made anything that wasn't born essentially luminous, you might need to repent. If you can't yet admit how lovable and infinitely worthy the fullness of your human nature is and if you think God wants to do anything but perpetually pour an abundance of love gifts upon you, well, my dear, your soul just might need to go to confession.

Sin is a distorted expression that reflects disconnect from the truth of our eternal beauty. Most often it is not punishment that needs to be administered so much as the beauty of our reality to be attuned to and affirmed.

To sin is to act incongruously with the wild grace of love. But there is no condemnation in that. This love doesn't abandon us with her scorn. Love is incapable of such things. We do, however, experience the natural suffering of dissonance when living outside of the harmonious, interconnected ecosystem of Life. This pain yearns not to punish—Nothing about Life is punitive—but to provide feedback that can aid us in reassessing our motivations that we might come closer to nourishing, sustainable relationship with existence.

Judgment is a crude, old-fashioned tool. Attraction to the beauty we might experience and contribute through harmonious relationship with ourself and our world is the paradigm that needs to be nurtured.

Sin is not a condemnation of character or any kind of lasting black mark. It comes from the misperception of experiencing yourself as being separate from love and acting out the pain of that.

The worst thing we ever did is put God in the sky, out of reach, pulling the divinity from the leaf, sifting out the holy from our bones, insisting God isn't bursting dazzlement through everything we've made a hard commitment to see as ordinary. The worst thing we ever did is strip the sacred from everywhere to put in a cloud-man elsewhere, prying closeness from your heart.

The worst thing we ever did is take the dance and the song out of prayer, made it sit up straight and cross its legs. We removed it of rejoicing, wiped clean its hip sway, its questions, its ecstatic yowl, its tears.

The worst thing we ever did is pretend God isn't the easiest thing in this Universe, available to every soul, in every breath.

PRAYER

— ✿ —

Speak to us of prayer. And *The Prophetess* spoke,

Let prayer bubble up in you, like water in a spring, like song in a bird, as a natural thing. And let your devotion be for the reception of your beauty and the fullness of your joy.

Your prayers needn't be small and meek. Let them also be large and gladsome. Why would we not ask for the natural gift of our greatness to be pulled forth from us like a tree from a seed? It wouldn't impress creation for a flower to hold back its blossom citing modesty as its reason. This world wants all of you, and you are filled with gifts to be brought forth, each carrying the name of one of your deepest joys.

A seed is in constant communion with the sun. The relationship between our hearts and an unconditional grace is just the same. There is beauty within us whose emergence Life yearns for. Prayer is planted in us that we may participate in our flowering. Prayer awakens and activates Life's intentions within us. It waters our sacred desires and germinates our destiny.

Whether or not the concept of God supports you, do pray. Prayer gives voice to your heart and mobilizes your great desires. Everything in this universe is energetically linked, and like an invisible root system, information and resources are shared. Our words are the ambassadors of our intentions to the Universe's Great Ears that exist everywhere. The sun and the bud have the same yearning, to bring the inner essence of the rose forward. Trust that the precious desires already folded into you, petal-like, are placed there to open. What if your truest, sweetest desires and that of The Great Wild Beloved might just be one? If this theory even might be true, that there's something generous and receptive about this universe and that channels open when we ask them to, well, any good scientist would be wise to experiment.

Whether or not you believe in the God you've been trained in, please pray for your own sake, great prayers of thanks that you may more closely experience Life. Pray prayers of thanks for the mountains, for the rivers, for the roundness of the moon just because they're here at all and because you get to know them.

Your body is a temple where your consciousness goes to pray. Go deep into yourself, into the land of reverent silence and praise *The Mystery* who created those curvaceous hills, those sumptuous valleys. Praise *Whatever* took the care to create the delicate origami of wildflower. Praise *She* whose attention to detail would allow light access to crawl through even the deepest tunnels of the Mariana Trench. Praise *That* which would have cared to fill the chests of birds with happy music. Praise *The Essence* who weaved the tapestry of this universe on that orbital loom and *She* who was wild enough to have slipped those dervish planets all that celestial wine to keep them whirling in eternal devotion around a splendid light. Praise *The One* who made circles and cycles and softness and yielding the rule, who paused to make the exquisite flowering of every living thing susceptible to light. Offer your thanks that each night a blanket of stars is spun for you—Praise invites a *Nameless Joy* to leap from your heart.

Every true prayer is the experiment, "Am I connected to any-thing larger than myself? Does anything larger that listens with attuned interest and benevolence care about what I most care about? Is this a receptive and responsive universe?" Prayer is the master key. The vibration of your expressed joy and longing can unlock all things. Pray fully, pray vulnerably, risk everything with your prayers.

To pray is to plug our longing into the universe's love. You have permission to reform your relationship with prayer until it truly nourishes you. You no longer have to pray as you were taught—Drink dark chocolate and let the moon sing to you. Let the ancestors dance through your hips at the slightest provocation. Go to the river and howl your ancient pain into the current. Ache, desire, say "*yes*" to your longing. You no longer have to pray as you were taught, but as the stars crawl onto your lap like soft animals at nighttime, and God tucks your hair behind your ears with the gentle fingers of Her wind, and a new intimacy is uncovered in everything, perhaps you'll realize you're finally learning how to pray.

RELIGION

Speak to us of religion. And *The Prophetess* spoke,

May religion be organized like a crystal, like a nautilus shell, like the golden ratio, like something that comes from the magnificence of Life and carries, embedded in its structure, the natural order of sacred reverence. May it be a less compartmentalized thing and more an integrated rhythm of our lives whose patterns organize themselves around the life breath of unconditional love.

Should religion be a part of your path, let it not invite you into a club or a compartment but into a wide territory in your heart where you join the church of all things. Ensure that it honors the opening, unlocking, and disarming of your deepest heart and that it praises, not stifles, the whispers of God within your inner knowing.

All religions are emanations from the one prism of love. Let religion be a tool of loveliness that invites your wholeness home. Find a temple whose bell rings within the universal human heart. And let its call to prayer inspire you to bow to the vastness within all you do not know. Let it restore the deep remembrance of your gratitude to be part of the sacred ecosystem of our Earth. And may it help you feel connected and welcomed into the cathedral of Life. May it help you more deeply receive the rains that christen you. And may it be a force that serves your true happiness that allows the forest or the flower or the mountain to be blessed sanctuaries so glad to receive you.

If religion be anything, let it be a trellis that supports the natural growth and opening of your joy. Let it affirm that since time immemorial, your soul has wanted for nothing and has always been drenched in light and prosperous with God.

And in that, let the soul not come to God as a beggar, from a place of depletion and scarcity but as a river to a sea filled with eagerness and the ecstasies that only reunion with one's entirety can bring.

Religion must bring your practices, your prayers, your thoughts, your deeds out of dissonance with your deepest truth. For the path of truth is the path of resonance and greater coherence with Life's symphony. Get closer to this ringing truth inside you. As you attune your life to it, the reeds of your soul will quiver, and the tone of your life will reverberate through the cosmos, and your life will chime with light. Your joys and God's joys will ring in glorious accordance that unlock troves of wonder held in the repository of the universe.

Let religion show you that each atom is a holy place and that no matter what we do, our life is an animated prayer becoming increasingly self-aware of the ecstasy of its devotion. May religion affirm for you again and again that you and every luminous thing share an origin story.

Insist that your faith not recreate the old, treacherous pattern of leaving its shadows out in the cold. Advocate for bringing our struggles and shames in to a warm, well-lit abode of embrace. Religion must house and feed our darkness to restore it with love's nourishment. This is how we make our religious communities ever more genuine, human, and whole. It is in the deep and continual embrace of shadows that religion finds deliverance and becomes a space that can truly serve the heart. May any savior complex held by any members continually bow before the most marginalized parts of their own hearts, to honor their lowliness and humble their arrogance.

Truly, religion is meant to be the community practice of reconnecting with the heart's intimacy.

Let all you don't know be your pastor, and let her teach you of your humility. Let religion guide you not only to a particular place of worship but to flee less the majesty of each moment that the humble door of your ancient heart be more willing to open to the wide beauty of the world.

Pray to be excommunicated from the ideology of the elite. Holy Writings must affirm that the term DNA is scientific jargon for "the Scripture of You" and that the scrolls of our beings are naturally inscribed with Life's unfurling wisdom that doesn't need to be vandalized by ideas that do anything but tell you, "Just as you are, you are God's absolute and eternal delight."

Let religion be the untying of old knots that once kept your soul hitched to rigidity and smallness. And let your doctrine be whatever comes from this great untethering as the soul's full range of movement is restored. Your soul is an ancient heritage of love songs from God. Find a way of worship that pledges allegiance to that. Find a way to worship that expresses your devotion for the borderless birthplace deep in your chest where beauty again and again takes her first breath.

GOD

— ❦ —

Speak to us of God. And *The Prophetess* spoke,

You don't have to believe in God, but please, collapse in wonder as regularly as you can. Try and let your knowledge be side-swiped by awe, and let beauty be so persuasive that you find yourself increasingly willing to lay your opinions at her feet.

If the word "God" comes with too many weighty associations that haven't made your heart lighter, experiment with giving God a new name. Find a name that doesn't need so much redemption, that isn't tied to history and old gravity in your heart.

Try calling God "*Life*," the inspired intelligence that sings through all form and adds poetry to the radiance of the moon. Call it that which attunes us to beauty. Call it the *Wild Grace* that encourages the sapling into the oak, that which coaxes the apple tree into the fullness of its blossom, the truth that redeems us from the fallacious notion that we could be anything but love. We want a God that delivers us into the grandeur and nobility of our deeply rooted joy—What else is worth yoking our life to?

If a notion of God feels more cage than key, more should than want, more authoritative than attractive, more death than Life, more weight than wing, try a way that carries a more mellifluous tone. Try calling it *"She"* who animates the ocean waves, who composes sunsets, who carves the great clay bowls of the valleys and uses the steady hands of time to raise the mountains. Call it *"Ancient Reality," "Inspired Intelligence,"* or *"the Magic Within Science."* Call it *"the Ecosystem of Light that Connects Us All."*

This is the age to lay down the old God of wrath and retribution, to lay down the fearful burdens in your heart that have kept you separate from yourself and without joy.

Claiming the agency to redefine God is claiming the agency to redefine your life. Redefining our relationship with God is the king-pin of the new paradigm. For God represents our highest value, what our life most deeply cares about and serves. We could consider God to be the authority of permission we grant ourselves that determines how deeply we'll accept ourselves, how bravely we'll shine, and how fully and truly we dare to live.

We've thought of God as being supremely disciplined, a master of morality, an enforcer of commandments. The truth is, She'll throw it all out again and again anytime She finds a quicker route to get to your heart.

Is God not the quality of relationship between you and all things? Is it not the light that rises like an invisible sea in the heart? And can the darkness that lands there also be treated as God? For if light has never hidden its face from any darkness, then what of its Creator?

This I know—There is a vast and intimate benevolence here. To surrender is to release our fears into that. To surrender is to release our blocks to receiving into that. And as we do, this benevolence becomes us, and we it, and eventually we see that nothing has ever ultimately been outside of this.

Our understandings of God are malleable—Why not adapt them until they resonate only with the tuning fork of love?

Have your first taste of love tonight for that Essence that made rainforests, water, trees, and time. Have your first taste of love tonight for that Essence of unimaginable intelligence that sang

stars and orbits and the immense collection of tiny perfec-
tions of all the creatures of the sea into being. Have your first
taste of love tonight for that Essence that was gracious and
giving and unimaginably tender enough to have created *you*.
To have thought you up and said, "Her. I want to see what her
blossom looks like. I desire her style of light." Have your first
taste of love tonight for that Genius of Love who makes flow-
ers ache toward light and hearts that do the same. Have your
first taste of divine love tonight—You might just say, "I want
more of that."

SUFFERING

Speak to us of suffering. And *The Prophetess* spoke,

Reflect on your life, asking, "Has not suffering been the greatest bearer of delivering my truest self to my awareness? Has it not been this devastating mercy that has husked me from illusion? Is it not, largely, suffering's hand that has delivered me to a deeper understanding of my gifts?" That suffering, too, can be among the finest tools to support our full becoming is a testimony to the great benevolence within existence. Look at this with clear eyes and it seems, then, that if suffering can be an ally to our deepest soul, then there is nothing to flee and even if our outer world appears to be laid to waste, hidden jewels can be found amidst our seeming wreckage.

Still, develop the discernment between the suffering that serves a small master and vandalizes the structure of all you're meant to be and the suffering that serves your truth and that carves you into all you're meant to be.

And should this great artisan, suffering, choose you to be its subject, say, "Sculpt me." And if you can, trust its hand—Its goal is to whittle away what no longer serves you and reveal the clear face of your beauty. Suffering is a clandestine sweetness. It chips the world off of you, reveals only God.

Be not entitled to thinking Life should conform itself to particularly pleasurable circumstances around you. And feel not a failure for the hard surprises and uncontrollable events that befall you. Suffering is a great emissary of awakening and there is no shame in her calling upon you to strip you of your collection of vain imaginings. She bears the parcel of humility to lay on the stoop of your heart. Receive it. Life's unsavory events can be the finest seasoning for your deepest becoming.

And as a grape ripens until it is ready to be crushed into wine, so, too, does your pain ripen within you until it is ready to be crushed into love. The missing ingredient for peace, as suffering ripens you toward love's obliteration, is trust in The Vintner's sacred timing.

Suffering burns through containments of our understanding and widens us to receive more of Life's mysteries and joys. In this sacred incineration that is sorrow, the pure face of our beauty becomes unveiled.

And if you seek wisdom, go not to a teacher, but into the mountain of suffering within your own heart. For inside that suffering, the monk of your loneliness has been living inside the monastery of your body, meditating on ways to transform you. Kneel by his feet and let him tell you in great detail of all the illusions he is certain you are not. Receive from suffering the generous alms of all you no longer need to uphold.

GRIEF

Speak to us of grief. And *The Prophetess* spoke,

In grief, our consciousness pans for gold in the dark waters of the wound, and we find unimaginable worth.

Grief is the comprehensive distribution of inbuilt medicine. It is the voice of healing rippling its reordering vibrations through your being. It is the loving, powerful flood of self-redemption and a reclaimed humanity that sweeps down old, oppressive structures within that once kept us confined. It is the restoration of imagination and possibility to the once contracted mind as through it, everything expands and opens.

Grief is a rite of passage that introduces you to the custom-made gifts awaiting you in the unknown. Grief is not pure sadness—It is the brave and beautiful disarmament of the soul. It is an astoundingly intelligent reordering of ourselves. It can be the ecstasy of the heart's homecoming as we release resistance to Life. Grief is a deeper plunge into the sea of oneness that lives within us. In grief, the human soul can make no finer translation of God's mighty song.

There are times you grieve everything at once—Your childhood, your partner, every bit of your old God, your mortality, your fleeting form, the pain of your small grasp on how to deeply and lastingly love. We grieve all the times we made safe bets with Life instead of moving toward what was alive and true. There are times we grieve every trick for controlling the Unknown and putting God in a headlock.

As we purge this paradigm of knowing only our partial self, know that each loss is a death and each death a wedding, as we simultaneously break up with the old relationships to ourselves and wed truer versions of the ravishing bride of the eternal heart.

Bring not your pity to the sacred ceremony of another's grief. But rather bring your deepest honor and celebration to this great room of a soul's bravery. Through their tears they shed the old world. Grief is not truly about loss, but about change. It is the touching, honoring and releasing of a pattern that held the containment of love. Your tears release you to encompass more of yourself. As you sit with one in grief, lay your reverence, respect, and gratitude upon the altar of your witnessing. You are on sanctified grounds. You've been let in to the temple of transformation. What a great privilege to witness the rawest expression of truth and grace flood another's body and renew the world from the inside out.

We work so hard to preserve familiar patterns in ourselves. Unprocessed grief is at the root of these patterns. We become attached to titrating the wild movements of God and give ourselves only small doses of Life. We make sure to measure out our contact with uncertainty and we schedule tidy, brief, and well-monitored visits with our hearts. Grief wants none of this. She is the dance of the wild-haired, authentic God who wants intimate contact with our wholeness and who cares nothing for keeping us small.

Grief is the most authentic prayer that simultaneously expresses and answers the soul's longing for deeper connection with itself.

Look at the rain clouds. They open their hearts fully to pour their restorative intimacies upon the earth. There is deep generosity in their relinquishment of form. And the receptive earth is so grateful to be their confidant. Her thanks are flowers.

Grief is an old language inside us, ancestor-deep. It is an unsung howl in our bones made of history's antique collection of longings and losses, an ancient scroll of our sorrow. Open it. Grief is our soul's journey back from long ago when we left the great homeland of our own heart. It closes this distance.

Open the chrysalis of your sorrow that has been silently growing your wings. Embodied release is the holy process of your remaking. Angels flock to you in your grief. Light migrates on its golden wings to your broken heart. Grace orients itself to your open sorrow.

In the temple of your deep tears, Life and death join voices inside of you in a chorus of unbearable beauty. The time of the end and the time of the beginning are both soluble in these deep tears. The house of the old that sheltered the temporary is honored and dismantled and the house of the new, made to hold more of the eternal, is simultaneously built.

There's a form of sacred crying that is the act of the true warrior. This deep crying allows you to dive into and beyond the dark. The echoes of these tears sing through the halls of generations, blessing the ancestors.

This deep crying purges the sickness of secrets. It is the honoring and ushering forth of the authentic that for so long felt it had to compromise itself for safety. It is the undoing of the body from being bound by the tyrannies of the past.

It undoes the corsets of worn-out contracts your soul never wanted to live in. This crying resuscitates your breathless life and is the embodied refusal to go on serving what no longer serves you. This deep crying is not a mere expression of sadness, but a cleansing of the deep heart, a purging of separation. Sacred tears are soul diamonds, 14-carat truths, God proposing marriage to your wholeness.

DEATH

Speak to us of death. And *The Prophetess* spoke,

That your heart is a small, beating, mortal thing is really a great mirage, an incredible sleight of hand. Inside you'll find an unfolding landscape of God—The mystery within moons, the grandeur within mountains and a limitless, limitless Love that could never be bound by anything so small as death.

Much of our life involves working around our fear of death. We need to recover from this. To avoid death is to avoid Life. On the other side of our fear of death, death and Life become indistinguishable.

One day, and really before long, your body will pass, and everything you've clung to and every way you've gained a name in this world will be laid to rest. Your hands will have become snags, no longer fruit-bearing, and Life will have written Her last signatures into the lines on your face. And everything that is real and true and alive in you now will still be real and true and alive in you then.

Death, if looked at rightly, has nothing to do with death but with how much we trust Life to hold us and carry us through and beyond the veils of our fears into the land of wider and more glorious reality.

For we find here that there is no true loss, only the deepest returning to the source of our luminosity. As we move through fears of death, energy becomes unbound that allows us to love more truly, more purely, more limitlessly. There is but one way to deeply kiss our lives—To recognize death as the great revealer of the utter futility to do anything but love.

Our fears of death lie not with what's out there, but are based in fearful, limited assumptions about what's inside of us. Unwilling to test that we might be more than mortal, crushable, extinguishable creatures, we frenetically move through life abandoning the possibility that we might be otherwise. We can tragically remain too out of touch with the realm of essence to confirm to ourself its endlessness.

The Beyond is a limitless realm that lives within. A synonym for death is Love beyond constraint.

For the sake of reality, meditate on your own death. Enter such close communion with your impermanence that you come out of your primary addiction to mortal life which makes us think we have to preserve everything at all costs. Meditate on the certainty of your death, the tone and curve and texture of its promise, and your soul will begin to purge itself of every fear-based motivation. For we hold fear to protect us from death, though with it, we ward off Life.

Our world is at a paradoxical time where we must die before we die or we will kill ourselves with our self-preservation. Hold each other and die consciously and beautifully to every limited thing we've imagined ourselves and the world to be.

Get as close as you can to death, which is to become intimate with the pulse of Life, and She will tell you Her vital secret: Everything that can be lost will be lost. But what can be lost is not everything. The path of losing everything is the path of discovering the eternal heart.

MARRIAGE

Speak to us of marriage. And *The Prophetess* spoke,

Let your vows be not a dogma to the dusty weight of *shoulds*, but living scripture that continually renews your tenderness.

Let your marriage be a growing structure for Life to evolve within you. May the gifts you give to your beloved be from Life herself that flower new knowings and wisdoms and kindnesses through you.

Should you choose to marry, know this is the commitment to the process of divine marriage in your own heart. Your dowry will be your willingness to successively move through your pain that stands in the way of you and this great union. But see not the movement through this pain as love's inconvenience or its obstacle but as that which matures its strength and develops its trustworthiness.

Remember to regularly renew your vows in the chapel of your open heart. And may your first commitment be to the continual dissolution of the idea that you could ever possibly claim the other, or that your understanding of them could ever be contained. Maintain close contact with the sacred unknowns in each other, for this is how to share a heart that is fresh with wonderment.

To build a steady abode of trust that can shelter the scope of two lives requires learning the great skill of how to ever more deeply bow. Though you may ever be an apprentice in love, stay dedicated to the ongoing craft of its mastery. And know that to bow deeply and truly, is to become the sky.

Do ask yourself the hardest questions before you make such a vow. Interrogate your motivations with the finest tool of your most scrupulous truth. Go into the great and lonely mountains of your soul and ask yourself how well you've come to know your own heart—For the depth to which you can hold yourself will be the depth to which you'll be able to lovingly hold the other. Ask yourself the mightiest question if your connection adds lightness to each other and moves on the wings of beautiful desire or if it's a laden thing, weighted with the deadening task of protecting the fears of your past. Assess if there's an eternity of longing in your chest to gift your partner ever new iterations of love.

Honor yourself by choosing a companion with whom sharing both your hardest and most beautiful truths will bring you closer. And know that intimacy, which is love's life breath, will be yours to the degree you desire to access and share your deepest, most disarmed truths with each other.

A partnership that is a wellspring of truthfulness will be a soaring and life-giving thing that rings with light. A marriage in which truth is stored away and silenced will be as an empty room or an unvisited cellar, cold and dusty with the unspoken.

Do all you might to make this sacred agreement a golden key and not a cage, that you may devote yourself to the continued liberation of more of each other's beauty.

Seek and cultivate a love that can blossom even as your bodies wither. Ensure you find a preciousness in yourself and in the other so deep and dear and lasting that no denial of aging or overlooking of the fleeting nature of form is required. And by this, your love will be given a great depth and a root in the eternal and will thereby source its sustenance.

Let your marriage be a home in which frailty and power, weariness and radiance can be received with equal hospitality. And continually furnish the space between you in a way that welcomes more and more of each other's hearts home. Should you hold in your heart the desire for marriage, give yourself the great gift of waiting until you find a jewel in another you must give your life to polishing.

DESIRE

Speak to us of desire. And *The Prophetess* spoke,

We did not come to this world to walk in a straight line. Bees dance to tell each other where the nectar is, and God slipped wine to the dervish planets to make them whirl in eternal devotion around their beloved orb of light. We did not come to this world to deprive ourself of sweetness and satisfaction. Observe the flowers who entirely undo their hiding with the greater impulse to share their beauty.

We did not come to this world in which seeds become towering trees and the Universe gleefully expands into Her own mystery to play small. Every bit of this world is so wild with desire to bring forth its love. Our hearts did not come to this world to stay tame.

The flower benefits from the hummingbird following her sweet desire for nectar. Darling, it's the same for us—All hearts will be pollinated by you following the honeyed river of your soul's desires.

Do not listen to the spirituality that has drably painted a value system that would discard desire for stoicism. True spiritual maturity has wisdom enough to never want to cast out the magnetic verve that pulls us toward custom designed sweetness. As we develop and root more deeply into ourselves, we become more attuned to Life's music playing through our quivering reeds with a wiser ear. Follow that music.

Desire can be a tarnished, tawdry thing if its pursuit is motivated by avoidance of an uncleaned wound. But this is not true desire. This is fear-based fleeing. True desire is deep listening to a clear stream of divine music that sings within you. To listen isn't to be immature or reckless but to be responsive to the call of Life.

Your ears are beautiful, tiny amphitheaters that can hold every dancing sound, those perfect singing bowls that softly pour music through you. Your eyes are fire opals, bejeweled drops of God, the translators of that great romance language of light. Your mouth is the soft, holy vessel from which every sacred sound is ushered forth, that hollow space that vibrates ideas into shape that gives form to love. Your nose is the host to that great visitor, the fragrance of the rose. Your skin is a landscape of sensation, a soft bed for touch that covers all of you at once. Dear ones, you were not given to this world to be rigid. For God's sake, we have tongues made of pure desire to devour and savor every sweetness. We live in a sensuous, perfumed world—Darlings, you were made to fall in love and this world was made to caress you.

Disown the small idea that we are not the sacred love child of the sea and the moon. Claim what you love. It's time to get fed. Pull God close and tell Her exactly what you want. Fling open the oceans in your heart and drink in the stars.

Once you start to heal all that old pain you came in with, the ancestors start hollering through your chest, "Now go fulfill your great desires."

JOY

Speak to us of joy. And *The Prophetess* spoke,

I want to speak with you about all the dazzling wonders our Universe is plotting on your behalf. Become quiet and eavesdrop on the secrets shared between the flower's heart and the sun, those intimacies that awaken the closed eyes of the bud to the astonishment of all this great light ever pouring on its behalf.

Come, let us stop pretending the stars are a tough crowd. Let us get on with remembering they're a wild, jovial audience in nighttime's great arena applauding and applauding with their golden hands the courageous stumble of our tender, earthly mess, all those forgivable things we get up to down here. Come, let us stop this lifeless practice of forgetting this world is a jewel-packed, orbed blessing. Rise each morning knowing there's a song of wonderment our Cosmic Composer sung into us that is ceaseless. Our hearts are ongoingly courted by a great, wild beauty. It's time we make a firm commitment to receive the resuscitation of our joy. Let us make a firm commitment to stop enabling these wild hearts to do anything but exactly what they've always wanted to do—To do anything but love.

And if your joy should become a distant, faded thing, I give you this prescription that each day before our surroundings become flat with familiarity and the shapes of our lives click into place dimensionless and average as Tetris cubes, say, "Wow." Before hunger knocks from our bellies like a cantankerous old man and the duties of the day stack up like dishes and the architecture of our basic needs commissions all thought to construct the four-door sedan of safety, say, "Wow." Before gravity clings to our skin like a cumbersome parasite and the colored dust of dreams sweeps itself obscure in the vacuum of reason, say, "Wow!" Each morning before we wrestle the world and our heart into the shape of our brain, look around and say, "Wow." Feed yourself fire. Scoop up the day entire like a planet-size bouquet of marvel sent by the Universe directly into your arms and say, "Wow!" Break yourself down into the basic components of primitive awe and let the crescendo of each moment carbonate every capillary and say, "Wow." And before our vision gets too veiled, let the sun stay a conflagration of homing pigeons that fights through fire each day to find us.

For what is this acumen we've developed to describe our terrors? Why are our stories of pain so well carved and whittled? Why these Ph.D. certificates of our errors hanging all over ourselves? No matter what the degree of joy, of beauty, why not give ourselves over to that? No matter how far we are from where we are aiming to go, why not look at it differently? Why not say, "I am light building a kingdom of myself"?

The deepest hope of happiness is to need no reason for itself. But if you do need a reason to allow yourself this most natural gift, let it be because birds throw themselves into the sky like a handful of winged seeds to go pollinate the South with music. Let it be that each evening the sun creates a symphony of color and the tones of your heart have the palette to match it. Let it be because you have two hands that can hold another's soft face and magical eyes with black holes in the middle of them that spend their whole lives pulling in all light and beauty. Let it be because even the winter snag is shimmering with secret promise and if you look with clear eyes you can see a hint of its hidden fruits.

Every bucket of your darkness is alchemized into wisdom simply by handing it to light. When we are born we are given an automatically refillable bag of jewels called a soul that we can share with any living thing to make it sparkle and sing. Joy is your essence and your birthright. Every beauty leaps from the spring of your open heart. All creation is made to laugh with you.

ANGER

Speak to us of anger. And *The Prophetess* spoke,

A seeker came to a wise woman and asked, "I want to awaken to my true nature of presence and love, but what do I do with all this anger?"

The woman said, "Awakening can be a vague and troubling path that leads many just about nowhere if it doesn't include your anger, if it doesn't include all of you."

If we reflect on our experience of separation, which is the cause of suffering, it doesn't come from nowhere. It comes from the mistaken notion that we need to judge ourselves into purity, whitewash ourselves with rejection—All of this is the path of conditional love, a fragmented relationship with self that will only partially satisfy. Paradoxically, it is our inability to be with our anger in full, accepting presence that densifies our anger and leads us to its mishandling.

Anger is a natural human emotion. Purify yourself as much as you like; it will likely still come. For it needn't be seen as a problem, a thug, a threat, treated as something unnatural to purge from ourselves. It is one of Life's many expressions and as we learn to be with it, listen to it, receive its wisdoms, it can give us profound gifts. It is only in the rejection of our feelings that they become hazards.

Anger is a vibrant life force that moves through us. Mostly, anger is mad about the narrative of its wrongness! As we exonerate anger from the narrative of wrongness, of outsiderness, that keeps it trapped and hurting and disenfranchised, it can mature you, clarify you and revitalize your life. Anger is a force that powerfully brings long-buried parts of us to light. When responsibly handled, we can think of anger as the brawn of love.

The path to awakening isn't transcending the self into dissolution, but embracing the self into love. And that includes your anger.

We don't want to sterilize our life with the spirituality of perfectionism. We want to learn how not to flee our experience and to learn how not to harm when we're hurting. What we find as we learn to stay with ourselves, which is the great skill of learning to responsibly feel, is that there is a gift and a wisdom in every emotion that moves through us when we don't repress it or project it but deeply receive it.

To be present does not mean to be present only with bliss. It means to stay in honest connection with whatever is arising within us. To learn to be present with the flame of our anger and stay in its burn rather than become a wildfire is one of the most powerful and valuable human capacities we can possess. When we let anger burn through us and feel it to its full resolution, we are purified, remade, and revealed. In this, all that doesn't serve Life turns to ash.

Anger protects a part of us that feels violated and that is not yet safe to express itself more vulnerably. When we try to silence anger, we take away our protector.

Let your anger be rooted in love. Love is where your power is. If you remember why you're angry and connect with what it more deeply longs for, your anger will be more effective, more creative and a force of construction rather than destruction. It matters what your anger serves.

Anger does not have to be violent. Anger can be the most liberating force available to us. One of anger's healthy and marvelous purposes deals with helping us to break out of oppressive patterns, which is to bring more of our truth home, into embodied expression.

Healthy anger is a tool for fortifying the system psychologically and emotionally to provide the necessary strength to bring ourselves out of internalized oppression—Ways of capitulating with external oppression. Violent anger is oppressive. It comes from and perpetuates separation. To oppress is to threateningly limit the expression of truth. Healthy anger is a redistribution of power, a restoration of truth, an inner advocacy for worth and wholeness, that propels us forward into more whole, just, and authentic ways of relating.

SHADOWS

Speak to us of shadows. And *The Prophetess* spoke,

This world is hungry for a deep light that can only be harvested through our shadows. Our souls are hungry for a spirituality that allows the full range of our authentic being, that doesn't insist on our shallow light while cutting the depths of our sacred darkness off at the knees.

Our hearts are hungry for a feeling of home that allows all of us back in, even and especially our most exiled and condemned parts, our most lawless and impoverished and impossible to control parts, our most disheveled and devilish and unkempt parts that have never known how to put themselves together.

You were very brave to have come to this world, a place where your light would not always be seen. We need to connect with the small, the contracted within us not as some laborious duty to our trauma or as a macabre idol of our past but because universes live in these places. When held in love, our shadows explode into worlds of new understanding.

The full moon once thought it had finally arrived, that it would stay whole this time. That it wouldn't wane anymore into darkness. And hasn't your heart thought the same thing right before another plunge into its necessary school of shadows? But to insist on staying light is unnatural and without elegance. Darling, learn the rhythms of descent into your darkness. The moon would be much less alluring, would have no message to teach, and her process would be far less poetic if she only knew the luminous side of her wholeness.

May we cease valuing an intimidating flawlessness and become generous in sharing our sacred wound. Forget perfection. Go for messy, learning, tender, whole. Forget brand new. Embrace cracked, broken open, worn, rich with story. Forget polished. Choose rusted, textured, nuanced, real. Forget divine—Try human.

Embrace your shadows and enter a new terrain of closeness in yourself. As we learn to embrace our shadow, we become moved by an authentic goodness that embraces our wholeness and has no opposite.

Open your heart and catch God kissing the devil, right there in the bedchambers of your chest. Let our judgments of good and bad that we've so placed at odds from each other finally rush into each other's arms and express the great affection that comes from their integration in one another.

Comedians need a space to cry, and spiritual leaders need a space to share their insecurities and how vulnerable they feel. Religious people need a space to share their doubts, and priests need a space to confess their desires. Mothers need a space to wail when we long to escape motherhood, and parents need permission to curl their hurts into fetal position and cradle their hearts. It must be okay for saints to also have scuff marks and for monks to long to come down from the mountaintop. Doctors need a space to talk about their addictions, and mystics must be allowed to also trudge through the mundane. We need to be able to tell God we hate Him now and then to stay in honest and whole relationship. To be fully human, we must be allowed to share our full experience of strength and struggle in a way that doesn't threaten our belonging. We must grow into hearts that can hold all parts of ourselves. For our light to go on sustaining itself, it must be allowed its shadow.

SENSITIVITY

Speak to us of sensitivity. And *The Prophetess* spoke,

No one has ever been too sensitive. The sensitive are frontierspeople of feeling, and sensitivity is where our power lives. The human spirit is sensitive. To be a sensitive person is to be attuned to the needs for its flourishing.

The sensitive ones are those who are brave enough to diagnose and call out this terrible malady of being so far from our own hearts. They are those warriors for whom to live lives contrary to the needs of the human spirit is an anguish and in that they are called to be creators of a new way.

We have crucified the sensitive for they see beyond the reaches of the veiled confines fear has placed on our vision. We have called the sensitive inconveniences to the mindless motions of our lives conducted by our historical unwillingness to feel.

To be sensitive does not mean to be moody, sullen, or easily wounded. It means you are a great translator of truth. It means you are a golden carrier of medicine for the parts of the world that have grown numb. It means you know we are here for love and you rightly feel the agony of our society's distance from this truth.

For the sensitive, the falsity of maintaining a facade can be unbearable. The sensitive are those who are especially equipped for the journey into the heart of intimacy where they can kiss the tender lips of God and come back to share these love secrets with the world.

The sensitive navigate the dissonance between Life's messages and the messages of our society and are here to close that gap. Unresolved pain callouses our sensitivity to the majesty of the finer brushstrokes of Life. Dear wise, sensitive ones, don't be so quick to pathologize yourself. How beautiful that your body speaks up so clearly as a barometer for truth, love, health, and safety and makes such a wild protest in their absence.

Why is it that so often the sensitive ones are the poets, the artists? Because, my dear, they are the ones tuned in enough *to hear the Universe.*

SURRENDER

— ❧ —

Speak to us of surrender. And *The Prophetess* spoke,

Like a rushing river, Life longs to flood its refreshment through your being and carve out the canyons of your past. It longs to stir up old sediment without judgment or guilt and carry it away on its impartial currents. Be clay in the hands of the seasons. Let them shape you as they please and see how little you can object to every twig and flower and frost-bite they mold into you. Be emptied of everything you know and think you know and pulse with that emptiness like our raw mass of earth before it was sophisticated into shape and name. Your prayers can be simple: "Grace, just let me know I'm here and that you're involved."

Our controlling ways are actually quite crude compared to the way grace works. Look how the Earth has let herself go and somehow the flower is drawn. Our willpower, all that efforting, is astoundingly weak compared to the easeful way beauty shares herself through the form of hummingbird. Our perfectionism is a rough attempt compared to the wild order of the leaf.

There is an elegance in timing that nothing can teach you so well as spring. The way she summons flowers open with the magical finesse of light, her touch never skipping over the face of even one buttercup. It's hard to trust the sun when you've been gone from her so long, I know, but spring is an internal season, her vitality is perennial, and she is not an abandoner. Be patient with your flowering, dear one; the agony of waiting is part of the blossom.

It's not our fear, our anger, our pain, our loss we can't bear. It's receiving love in its fullness. For that is our final surrender, our death, the laying down of our control. It's what baffles every strategy in the mind that wanted to think itself so impressive in its myriad ploys. Every drama we play out is the skittish hesitation before the door to love's great temple. The one question lovers should ask themselves is, "How deeply am I willing to let love subsume everything in its way on the path to my heart?"

Surrender says, "Put me amid Life's simplest things that give their lives to blooming without reaching for a name. Position my gratitude such that my heart gets much of its needs met from sunlight and open me in a way that I may receive the deep communion and nourishment of silence. God, remove from me all obstacles that I may remember the great laughter that I am. May I settle into belonging here in the humble majesty of the verdant, breathing cathedral of this Earth. May I want for no spiritual mastery but to be porous like the soft Earth to the rain and to receive whatever amount of grace this small heart is able to bear."

Surrender asks that you never again attempt the arrogance of trying to conquer another's heart, but rather become a great ally to its freedom. This is surrender's prayer: "Dear God, if you please, no more of this distance. Plant yourself in my body. I want nothing but to be alive with the movements of Wild Grace."

SELF-WORTH

Speak to us of self-worth. And *The Prophetess* spoke,

Be done with small, meek prayers. There is a surging ocean of light within you—Ask that it flood the world. Enough gifts have been placed within you to satisfy eternity. Ask that they be brought forth and unwrapped. Be done playing small. Ask that your voice soar high enough to kiss the sun and come back to share her stories of light with the world. Why think it unseemly to ask precisely for the vastness of desires that have been placed in your chest to show themselves? We are temples holding the Great One. Would it not bring joy to all creation to make the mysteries and delights of our Universe reveal themselves through you? You are the boldness of the universe that knows its potential is uncontainable. Be ready to expand into wondrous realms of your Self. Be ready to receive the great astonishment of all you might unfold to be. Put yourself forward and see how Great Beauty might rise to meet you.

We must reframe this fear of being "too much." We contain the universe and must practice receiving all that we are. Go forth, glorious too much ones, and pour your rivers of light that quench the world. Go forth and feed every ravenous soul from the generous table of your heart knowing your essence is one of feast, not famine. Go forth and live in a way that reminds people how abundantly luminous each night is, bedecked in her stars. Let your too muchness be your devotion—God, after all, is the Queen of Too Much, polyamorous with every religion and every heart as She is and She does not stop making Her point after only one galaxy. Your heart was made to be a gong, not a penny whistle. Your beauty is a downpour, not a sprinkle. Your voice is a nourishing meal for this hungry world, not a garnish. "You're too much" has been a tight judgment that tries to tie down your vastness and constrain the cosmos within you—Reclaim it and pour forth your stars; reclaim it and become just the right size to hold the Universe.

CREATIVE EXPRESSION

Speak to us of creative expression. And *The Prophetess* spoke,

The world needs your voice. The voice that emerges from the depths, that comes from listening to whatever is alive in your depths.

You have permission to say anything.

Step from the robe of your facade and show your truth to us, trembling. Whatever your creative block, dip your pen into the heart of its reasons and tell about that: about the flatlands with no topography of inspiration you've been wandering down for so long, about how muse seems to be an endangered species—Let us feel your drought of God.

Tell us about the curvature of the ice block of your numbness and all the factors that have carved its shape. Tell us of your affairs with loneliness and how you can't seem to stop returning to her cold bed. Talk about the artists you're jealous of, how all you want to do is sign your name to their flame. Show us the graveyards in your heart filled with all the beloved things you've lost. Don't just give us pictures of the bathed, swaddled baby—the tidy aftermath—We want to know the pangs of how you've birthed yourself or aborted this process time and time again. Yearning is the siren that summons the writer—Sing us her song. Writing has nothing to do with crafting perfect, calligraphed words—Grab the inkwell and spill your truth. A poem is where the flint of soul strikes the stone of trauma and makes a spark. A poem is a thumbprint of the soul. The page wants you to leave your evidence. The world needs your voice. Unsheathe your knowing. *You have permission to say anything.*

Artists of the deep heart are not apart from suffering. Inspiration comes from kneeling down far enough to kiss even the deepest wound. Don't do the unnatural thing of separating the sacred from its sorrow. The great artists have learned the craft of melting it into gold. They don't flee from suffering— They make its fire their medium.

The arts are perhaps the finest vehicle for the awakening of human consciousness. Through the arts, Truth is not delivered only conceptually to the mind, which yields a superficial or partial level of understanding. With its intricate, intelligent, and evocative diplomacy, elevated art can reverberate open a receptivity to new dimensions of understanding in its recipients.

Shine your eyes, see the beauty of things, and tell it like it is. To tell it like it is is to awaken yourself to reality. Multiple stanzas are written in every petal, buckets of inspiration drip from the dewdrop and reams of heart-opening poetry glisten in each direction light turns her head. What is creative expression if not going outside, or deeply into yourself, and simply telling it like it is?

If you feel creatively dry, or should you get hung up on wondering if your creation is worthy or if it has already been done, remember, the moon longs to whisper the intimacies of her radiance to you. The silver rivers want you to learn to read their calligraphy, and the stars long to include you among their scribes. The burgeoning desires of spring long to make your heart their confidant. Cover the song of the world saying its last words to summer's soft face. Autumn wants you to translate the vermilions of her melancholy. The truth in humanity's undercurrents has long been trying to sweep in your pen to write of this wild flow. Our unique creative expression is a deep service and an essential nutrient to the world. Give it.

The world performs its ablutions with the light of your creative expression.

FORGIVENESS

Speak to us of forgiveness. And *The Prophetess* spoke,

Forgiveness says, "I have been so cruel, I can now forgive most all in you. I have seen cruelty's true face as a frightened protector of wounded tenderness. I have seen such profound helplessness and insecurity inside of myself, I can now easily find the yet-uncovered dignity waiting within yours. I have felt so much humiliation in my own chest, I now want to lay flowers of deep understanding at the feet of all the hard work I know your pride must do. I've come to see your shadows as the poorest salesmen trying to sell you off for much less than you are clearly worth. I've rent so many veils asunder, suffocated with illusion as I was, I now have something of x-ray vision—Darling, there is little in you anymore that can convince me away from your untarnishable light."

The roots of most malice are made of an inhospitality to love learned from some great vacancy in our childhood.

Forgiveness is the rehabitation of love to the cold, empty rooms within us where we were taught love must be denied.

We must know the caverns inside of ourselves to forgive. We must be intrepid shadow sherpas willing to navigate the harrowing slopes all the way to the other side of our sorrows where we open to the wide view of truer perspective.

Forgiving another is secondary. Primarily, forgiveness has to do with resolving pain in ourself rather than storing it as armor. In true forgiveness we come through the other side of our pain with a more resourced, wise, and fortified love.

Crown your old wounds with the discovery of their innocence. When sorrow's closed bud comes to know itself, forgiveness is its blossoming.

Forgiveness is not an interpersonal nicety overlayed upon our unresolved pain. Forgiveness is an embodied transmutation and renewal of an old way of relating.

So much of our life energy goes into protecting and maintaining our emotional illnesses. We hold grudges whose hurt we perpetually blame when we don't know our hurt can heal. To forgive is to experientially understand that we are equipped to heal any emotional, psychological, or relational wound and that there is profound, incomparable, and strengthening value in being accountable for our own healing.

Forgiveness has nothing to do with a relinquishment or a corrosion of boundaries. As we move through the embodied, pain-purging process of forgiving, we restore ourselves with natural life-affirming boundaries that come from landing more fully in our loving strength. In this we release the effort to uphold those cruder protections of emotional weaponry.

If there's something inside of you you're still warring with, it simply means you haven't yet fully connected with the innocence at its root. Connection with this sweet, inbuilt medicine, at the base of even the greatest hostility, heals and informs all sorrow and delivers you into compassion's soft arms.

Self-forgiveness is the beginning of the end of violence ruling you. What we don't forgive of ourself becomes our own war. Forgive yourself. All of your faults have a root in something tender.

Begrudge yourself of nothing. Darling, there is no part of your process from tight, hard seed to full-petaled bloom that isn't deeply sacred. Every stage of the flower is an expression of progressive enlightenment. Flood yourself with forgiveness and drink in every part of yourself—You are The Beloved's unfolding prayer.

TRANSFORMATION

◆

Speak to us of transformation. And *The Prophetess* spoke,

To the God who does not make all of us famous, to She who is not an enabler of the great dreams of the grapes that instead they may be crushed into wine. To She who does not want to grant the coal deliverance from its suffering just yet, for somehow She sees within it the makings of unimaginable diamonds. To She who does not respond to the caterpillar's prayers to be all that it can be and instead makes it devour itself to bring forth the latent wings it otherwise never would have known. To She who impoverishes every illusion we thought was so precious. To She who steals our outer fortunes that would have made our hearts poor. To She who shows us our inner riches more magnificent and abundant than anything the external could have crowned us with. To She who steals every smallness on which I've hung my name—Thank you, from whom I will become.

Feel God germinating the seed of your heart again, new life bursting out through you and breaking down all that you've known that She may have more space to love the world through you.

My dear, resist nothing of the brief, exquisite experience of yourself. Why not enter the blaze of your sorrow, your joy now and see what it will allow you to become?

Transformation is the journey from fragment to wholeness. We must love freedom enough to embrace confinement. We must adore the ecstatic enough to integrate the mundane. We must be so inebriated with joy that we welcome all sorrow. We must be so desirous of wholeness that all our fragments reunite. We must yearn for home with such a yearning that our exiled pieces may return. We must love transcendence enough to allow the truth that transcendence is inclusive of all prior limitations. Your open heart remembers its brokenness. The blossom does not shun the bud.

What if we told the flower, "Don't bloom" and told the birds, "Don't sing" and told the petals, "Don't you dare show your tenderness" and told the bee, kissing the sweetest part of the rose's heart, "It's uncomfortable to see love given so freely" and told the stars, "Don't shine; it'll make someone scared" and told the quivering bunny trembling beneath shivering winds, "Toughen up" and told the clouds watering the Earth with their open heart, "Don't cry" and told the morning sun shining over slowly waking hills and enlivening everything, "Stop showing off" and told the music within the wind to "Keep its voice down"? These are the stories that have been told to our souls. The revolution is the liberation from and complete remaking of these narratives.

We are the mythmakers, our lives are pens, drawing with our movements, our steps, our actions the stories we're hoping to record into the world. What are the styles of relating we hope to inscribe? What is the tone of our presence here as we walk this soft earth?

Women, what stories do we want to tell about ourselves, about our sisterhood, our strength?

Men, what stories would you like to tell about gentleness and power co-existing?

Humanity, what stories would we like to tell about the great courage it takes to love, about the grand journey of finally opening our hearts to return to each other?

It's time to put our hearts together and consider: *How beautiful dare we make this world?*

THE TIME OF
THE BEGINNING

My friends, the tide is receding. The ocean is calling me back into its depths. It is time for me to go, yet this time I shall not sail away and leave you. Though, nor shall I, in the same way, return. It is time to make the great sacrifice that is to make all of us infinitely more sacred. It is time to let me go in form.

I am a light you cannot lose. I am a power in you that cannot be dethroned. I am a force that cannot be weakened. And I will abide in each of you forever. The sun of my dominion will not set. It is the idea that I could be separate from you that you will release, the idea that I have not forever lived within your chests.

You will find me in yourself, and in this claiming, I will burn brighter. I am the torch in your hips, the knowing in your heart. I am the connection in your solitude. I am the wisdom in your wound. I speak within you as the clearest voice of your inextinguishable light. The old way is done. This is the time of the beginning. Raise this torch and find me as you proclaim your light. Find me in each other.

Carry me in your difficulties, in your losses, in your loneliness. Carry me when you go through the crucible of learning to forgive someone. Carry me as you grieve yourself into deeper completion. Carry me as you strive to instate in the throne of your heart a truer God who can celebrate all of you. Carry me as you transform your arrogance into humility. I want to be integrated in you as you long to be integrated in me. Your reclamation of this light is the culmination of my wisdom. Raise your torches. Move as one.

Humanity has entered a process from which there is no returning. We are being impelled into the Unknown by an increasing need for authentic connection. The suffering of separation is in rapid acceleration, and from it, our desire for deliverance is moving us toward the great edge of the new, before a vast and comprehensive recognition of our oneness. Enough of us have said yes to this process, which has quickened this momentum.

We are at a tipping point where we can no longer be strangers to our own hearts. It is imperative that we learn to feel. It is imperative that we learn to welcome our deepest tears. It is imperative that the bravery it takes to shed them is unshakably known.

This is the age in which our voice, our intuition, our truth's clear song, our inner power, our inspiration, our deep guidance, our feelings, our humanity are being unburied from our bodies. This is the resurrection of our wholeness.

The end of investing in separation is coming. The end of participation in the needless re-creation of blame is coming. The death of fame is coming. The death of the myth of white superiority and male superiority, of spiritual superiority, of wealthy and educated and beautiful superiority is coming. The death of anything that crawls with the undercurrent of the insidious delusion *"I am better than you"* is coming. This blessed, long-awaited breakdown is coming. This great exporting of pain we've all been acting out on each other—We're beginning to hear its death rattle. The trumpet blasts are the end of the era of control. Your hands, your hearts, your visions, your intentions are being summoned to help pull back the dark veil over humanity's consciousness and birth the dawn. The time of the end has arrived. Hallelujah.

ACKNOWLEDGMENTS

To the essentialists, my pack of soul-mates who nourished my being, held me in grief, cheered on my wings and who have been my heart's home during the making of this book: Lucy Grace, Sheri Horvat, Venka Payne, Iliana Maura. You have witnessed and supported the most expansive and humbling chapter of my life. My gratitude for you is without circumference.

To my mom and dad, Rene and Bill Weiler. Bottomless love, bottomless thanks.

For my brother and sister, Hayden and Denali and my sister-in-law and brother-in-law, Elena and Luke.

For these creative wizards and geniuses in their various ways that have majorly inspired me, Alanis Morissette, Brené Brown, Elizabeth Gilbert, Vince Gilligan, Bryan Cranston, and J.B. Smoove.

To my beautiful children, Amari and Nahanni. You are the sun 'round which my adoration orbits. I am ever in awe. Thank you for being my children. Thank you for being exactly who you are.

To Asa, my spirit baby in the beyond. I love you.

To my mother-in-law, Janet Lipsey. Deep love. Deep thanks.

To Mary Reed, a blessing and a jewel in my life. Thank you.

To Noah Harkin, my soon to be ex-husband. Thank you. Here for you always.

To Eric Weiner, you are more a golden rope than a golden thread. Thank you for your friendship, support, encouragement and for the cigars over the years.

To Daniel Ladinsky. That I'm including you in my acknowledgments, that you wrote the foreword to this book, that you are in my life not just as an inspiration but also as a friend is a treasure still too valuable to properly understand.

To Thomas Stern. We sensed there was some creative collaboration in store for us. That it has taken the form of this book as author and illustrator is both magical and extraordinary, and also makes complete sense.

To my friends Okoree Peyralans, Tara Peyralans, Brook Maurer, Justin Larson, Nomi Summa, Astrid Schute—thank you.

To Terry, Jonathan, and Mike, my Illuman brothers, supporters, dear friends. I love you guys.

To August Jenson, my wise therapist. You've supported me so much, with such skill and kindness. You're one of a kind.

To Shamina Vahedi, energy worker, ancestral clearer, encourager, friend.

To Dan Geiger, hypnotherapist and friend. I'd be up some kinda creek without your transformational support.

To Doug Miller, my English teacher, a poet inspiration, and a deep support in my life. Thank you for saving my ass with your support during the editing phase of this book.

To my editor, Allison Janice. To work with someone so skilled, professional, encouraging, and down-to-earth has been a relief, a joy, and an edification. Thank you for trusting this book and bringing it into the fold.

To my beloved horseshoe at Path of Love: Nirodha and Puni, Kapi, Kasi, IO, Christina, Katia, James. Thank you for seeing me. Thank you for letting me see you.

There are many more dear friends, inspirations, and supports not mentioned here for whom I feel a depth of appreciation and gratitude.

Finally, I thank my A-Team, my Dead Poet Society—Kahlil Gibran, Hafez, Brian Doyle, and Saint Francis of Assisi.

ABOUT THE AUTHOR

Chelan Harkin's poetry journey began at age 21 on the heels of a traumatic event, a mystical event and an unparalleled creative opening where inspired verse started to pour through her without the need for editing. Her experience with channeling the muse was profound and intimate but also quite private. It took Chelan 12 years to find the courage to share her poetry with the world through her first self-published book, *Susceptible to Light*.

This publishing journey that began at the end of 2020 has been something of a magic carpet ride characterized by prayer experiments gone right. It has included some of the most awe-inspiring events that have been cosmically bonkers and completely shifted Chelan's way of relating to herself and the world. Along with *The Prophetess*, her current published books include *Susceptible to Light, Let Us Dance!: The Stumble and Whirl with The Beloved*, and *Wild Grace*.

Chelan grew up in the Baha'i faith, a minority religion that views all religions as coming from the same divine source. It describes this era, in the arc of human evolution, as the age in which humanity will have a major leap in consciousness through a deeper realization of our inherent oneness. Many of the inspiring perspectives from the Baha'i writings continue to influence Chelan's thoughts, life and writing. Curiously, Kahlil Gibran, author of *The Prophet*, was also closely inspired by the Baha'i writings.

Before her writing career took off, Chelan worked for 10 years as a hypnotherapist. She was fascinated by this healing modality through which she'd experienced profound transformational shifts. During that decade, Chelan dove deep into the world of understanding the subconscious mind and its powers and potentialities.

Chelan is 35 years old and lives in the Columbia Gorge, a scenic patch of earth in South Central Washington State, with her beautiful six- and three-year-old kids, Amari and Nahanni. Aside from writing and snuggling with her babes, her other loves include hiking, singing and making pretty decent dry comedy videos.

Since this publishing journey began, Chelan has traveled the country as an inspirational speaker, talking about mysticism

as the path of opening the heart to embrace our wholeness—
the wounds and the wisdom, the pain and the possibility.
Reach out to her with speaking invitations; she likes those.
That her life includes being the author of *The Prophetess*
brings Chelan far-reaching joy and unspeakable gratitude.

To learn more about Chelan and her work, visit her online at:
chelanharkin.com

Hay House Titles of Related Interest

YOU CAN HEAL YOUR LIFE, the movie,
starring Louise Hay & Friends
(available as an online streaming video)
www.hayhouse.com/louise-movie

THE SHIFT, the movie,
starring Dr. Wayne W. Dyer
(available as an online streaming video)
www.hayhouse.com/the-shift-movie

***

MADE OF RIVERS by Emory Hall

ANCESTORS SAID: 365 Introspections for Emotional Healing,
by Ehima Ora

RAID ON THE INARTICULATE, by Deepak Chopra

FINDING LOVE EVERYWHERE:
67 1/2 Wisdom Poems and Meditations, by Robert Holden, Ph.D.

THE MUSE TAROT: A 78-Card Deck and Guidebook, by Chris-Anne

All of the above are available at your local bookstore, or may be ordered by visiting:

Hay House USA: www.hayhouse.com
Hay House Australia: www.hayhouse.com.au
Hay House UK: www.hayhouse.co.uk
Hay House India: www.hayhouse.co.in

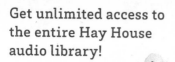